Family Tree
Mojisola Adebayo

T0347992

methuen | drama
LONDON • NEW YORK • OXFORD • NEW DELHI • SYDNEY

METHUEN DRAMA
Bloomsbury Publishing Plc
50 Bedford Square, London, WC1B 3DP, UK
1385 Broadway, New York, NY 10018, USA
29 Earlsfort Terrace, Dublin 2, Ireland

BLOOMSBURY, METHUEN DRAMA and the Methuen
Drama logo are trademarks of Bloomsbury Publishing Plc

First published in Great Britain 2023

Cover image: Pete McGlynn

Cover design: Solution Group

A catalogue record for this book is available from the British Library.

A catalog record for this book is available from the Library of Congress.

ISBN: PB: 978-1-3504-1653-6
ePDF: 978-1-3504-1654-3
eBook: 978-1-3504-1655-0

Series: Modern Plays

Typeset by Mark Heslington Ltd, Scarborough, North Yorkshire

To find out more about our authors and books visit
www.bloomsbury.com and sign up for our newsletters.

Actors Touring Company, in co-production with Belgrade Theatre
Coventry and in association with Brixton House, present

Family Tree

CAST

Henrietta Lacks	Aminita Francis
Ain (also plays Anarcha and Oshun)	Mofetoluwa Akande
Bibi (also plays Betsey)	Keziah Joseph
Lyn (also plays Lucy)	Aimée Powell
Smoking Man	Alistair Hall

CREATIVE TEAM

Playwright	Mojisola Adebayo
Director	Matthew Xia
Set & Costume Designer	Simon Kenny
Lighting Designer	Simisola Majekodunmi
Composer & Sound Designer	Francesca Amewudah-Rivers
Movement Director	Diane Alison-Mitchell
Associate Director	Amelia Thornber
Costume Supervisor	Maybelle Laye
Production Dramatherapist	Wabriya King
Tour Casting Consultant	Matilda James CDG
Original Casting Consultant	Sophie Parrott CDG

PRODUCTION TEAM

Production Manager	Matt Ledbury
Company Stage Manager	Cassie Adey
Deputy Stage Manager	Eliott Sheppard
Lighting Associate	Tom Lightbody

ATC is:

Artistic Director & Joint CEO	Matthew Xia
Executive Director & Joint CEO	Andrew Smaje
Admin Director	Juliana Bearse
Associate Producer	Melina Barnett
Finance Director	Kate Sarley
Chair of Trustees	Geraldine Brodie
Vice-Chair	Alan Evans
PR	Diana Whitehead, Fourth Wall PR

Acknowledgements

ATC would like to thank the many collaborators and colleagues who have helped to develop and realize this project. Co-producers Corey Campbell and Laura Elliot at Belgrade Coventry, Gbolahan Obisesan and Ruth Hawkins at Brixton House, who have joined us to make the national tour in 2023. Co-commissioners Young Vic Theatre, in particular Kwame Kwei-Armah and Despina Tsatsas. The team at Greenwich + Docklands Festival who co-produced a work-in-development, outdoor performance in August 2021, in particular Bradley Hemmings and Ellie Harris, and the cast, creative and production team of that early iteration of the play, which went on to win the Alfred Fagon Award for Best New Play.

ATC wish to thank Abcam (*www.abcam.com*) for their generous support, especially: Miguela Gonzalez, Hannah Tweddle, Danielle Norby and Alan Hirzel. Also, Henrietta Lacks Foundation for their warm support and advocacy. Please support them in return: *www. henriettalacksfoundation.org*

Mojisola Adebayo wishes to thank Matthew Xia, Andrew Smaje, Ameera Conrad and everyone at ATC then and now, Kwame Kwei-Armah (Young Vic), Bradley Hemmings (GDIF), the creative and production team who worked with us in 2021, Pathways Director Steven Reed, our anonymous sponsor and the extraordinary actors who contributed to the development of the play, namely: Michelle Asante, Diana Yekinni, Keziah Joseph, Natasha Cottriall, Alisha Bailey and Ronke Adekoluejo. *Family Tree* was written during a Research Fellowship, with thanks to Professor Dr Anja Schwarz and colleagues at the Institute of English and American Studies at Potsdam University. Thanks also to the School of English and Drama, Queen Mary, University of London and Professors Caoimhe McAvinchey, Dominic Johnson and the late, dearly missed and loved, Catherine Silverstone for supporting my research leave; the Lacks Foundation for their blessing on this play and the Alfred Fagon Award, 2021. Thank you to Natasha Davies and Counterpoint Arts for supporting me through the commission *Leaves from Family Tree*, giving me an opportunity to play Henrietta Lacks and develop workshops around the themes. *Family Tree* was first co-produced by Actors Touring Company with Belgrade Theatre in association with Brixton House. Thank you to Corey Campbell and all of these organizations and individuals for their support.

The author wishes to extend a further personal thanks to: Matthew Xia for developing the idea for this play, his incisive questions, artistry and inspiration for several lines; all the artists including actors who have given feedback and contributed towards this play; Dr Nicole Wolf for her enduring love and support in influencing the tone and place of the prologue, introducing me to permaculture, co-developing/facilitating the Agri/cultural Practices workshops and teaching me organic gardening alongside Åsa Sonjasdotter, Asmelash Dagne and Alfred Decker; the students at Potsdam and all the Agri/cultural Practices workshop participants and Timo Galbenis-Kiesel at Havel-Kranich; my dear brother-friend-collaborator and some-time agent Debo Adebayo; all my beautiful family of friends who came to see the work-in-progress performances at GDIF and gave me such support and encouragement; Dr S. Ama Wray for giving me a copy of *The Immortal Life of Henrietta Lacks* by Rebecca Skloot and telling me I should write a play; Dr Carole Jones for introducing me to Toni Morrison's *Beloved*, all those years ago, all the authors (named in my footnotes) who inspired and informed my research; Dr Rita Das for that powerful speech during Covid and everyone who treated me with such kindness in the NHS, with an extra special thanks to Umar, for simply being a dream come true.

Finally, this play was written in loving memory of Joyce Meggie, who nourished me as a child with Jamaican soul food, welcoming me as if I was one of her own and looked out for me in the hard times. You are always remembered. With love and comfort to her beloved daughters, Sonia and Natasha, and all your family. Thank you.

National Tour 10 March–17 June 2023

Venues: Belgrade Theatre, Coventry; Traverse Theatre, Edinburgh; Brixton House, London; Tron Theatre, Glasgow; Liverpool Everyman; Theatre by the Lake, Keswick; Theatre Royal Plymouth; Sheffield Theatres; The North Wall Arts Centre, Oxford; Nottingham Playhouse; New Wolsey Theatre, Ipswich; Tobacco Factory Theatre, Bristol.

Production History

Family Tree is a co-commission from Actors Touring Company and Young Vic Theatre. The play was first produced by ATC and Greenwich + Docklands Festival as a work-in-development 27–30 August 2021, with performers Michelle Asante, Natasha Cottriall, Keziah Joseph, Diana Yekinni; creative team Sandra Falase, Vicki Igbokwe, Ameera Conrad, Imogen Brown and Francesca Amuwedah-Rivers; production team Clementine Seely, Rachel Head, Catherine Mizrahi, Rhea Jacques and Lateef Salvador Oshinowo.

MOJISOLA ADEBAYO (BA, MA, PhD, FRSL, FHEA) is a playwright, performer, director, producer, mentor, workshop facilitator and teacher who has been making theatre for social change, internationally, for over thirty years, from Antarctica to Zimbabwe. Mojisola's own plays include *Moj of the Antarctic: An African Odyssey* (Lyric Hammersmith); *Muhammad Ali and Me* (Ovalhouse); *48 Minutes for Palestine/Oranges and Stones* (Ashtar Theatre, Ramallah); *Desert Boy* (Nitro/Albany Theatre); *The Listeners* (Pegasus Theatre); *I Stand Corrected* (Artscape, Cape Town); *The Interrogation of Sandra Bland* (Bush Theatre); *Wind/Rush Generation(s)* (National Theatre: Connections); and *Nothello* (Belgrade Theatre, Coventry). *Family Tree* won the Alfred Fagon Award for Best Play of 2021. Publications include *Mojisola Adebayo: Plays One* and *Plays Two* (Oberon Books); *The Theatre for Development Handbook*, co-written with John Martin and Manisha Mehta (Pan Arts); and *Black British Queer Plays* and *Practitioners: An Anthology of Afriquia Theatre*, co-edited with Lynette Goddard (Bloomsbury Methuen Drama). Mojisola teaches at Queen Mary, University of London, is an Associate Artist of Black Lives Black Words, AICRE, Pan Arts, the Building the Anti-Racist Classroom collective and an Honorary Fellow of Rose Bruford College. At the time of writing, Mojisola is on a research fellowship at University of Potsdam, Germany and is a Writer-on-Attachment to the National Theatre (UK). Mojisola's new play *STARS* (Tamasha Theatre Company/ Institute of Contemporary Arts) was shortlisted for the George Devine Award 2022 and premieres at the ICA in London in April 2023, before a national tour. See mojisolaadebayo.co.uk for more.

MATTHEW XIA, one of the busiest and most exciting directors in the UK, was appointed Artistic Director of Actors Touring Company in November 2018. He is a former Associate Artistic Director of Royal Exchange Theatre, Manchester; Director in Residence at Liverpool Everyman & Playhouse; and Associate Director of Theatre Royal Stratford East.

Some of Matthew's acclaimed productions include: *Frankenstein* and *Into the Woods* (Royal Exchange, Manchester); *Wish List* (Royal Exchange, Manchester/Royal Court Theatre); *Blue/Orange* and *Sizwe Banzi Is Dead* (Young Vic); *One Night in Miami...* and *Shebeen* (Nottingham Playhouse); and *The Wiz* (Hope Mill).

Matthew's most recent projects include *Feeling Afraid as if Something Is Going to Happen* by Marcelo Dos Santos (Francesca Moody,

Edinburgh Fringe First Winner, 2022) and *Hey Duggee* (Cuffe & Taylor, Kenny Wax, BBC Studios, national tour December 2022–June 2023).

Other work of note includes: *Blood Knot* (Orange Tree Theatre); *Sleeping Beauty* (Theatre Royal Stratford East); *Scrappers* and *Migration Music* (Liverpool Everyman & Playhouse); *Dublin Carol* (Sherman Theatre, Cardiff); and NitroBeat's *Suckerpunch Boomsuite* (Barbican).

Under the pseudonym Excalibah, Matthew was the first DJ to join BBC 1Xtra, where he spent six years. As a sound designer and composer, credits include: *The People Are Singing* (Royal Exchange, Manchester); *Freerun* (Udderbelly); *That's the Way to Do It* (TimeWontWait); *Bolero Remixed* (New London Orchestra). In 2012 Excalibah performed as a headline DJ at the London Paralympic Opening Ceremony.

Matthew is a founding member of Act for Change, a trustee of Artistic Directors of the Future, Cardboard Citizens and Get Into Theatre, and has served on the boards of Rich Mix, Creative Futures and Theatre Royal Stratford East. He has been a judge for the Bruntwood Prize for Playwriting (2017), the Yale Drama Series (2018), the Alfred Fagon Award (2017–21) and the Eurovision Song Contest (2022).

AMINITA FRANCIS

Theatre credits include: *Red Riding Hood* (Liverpool Everyman); *I Am Kevin and Babel* (Wildworks); *Frankenstein: How to Make a Monster* (Battersea Arts Centre); *The Immersive Great Gatsby* (Hartshorn-Hook Productions); *Josephine* (Theatre Royal Bath); *Bugsy Malone* (Lyric Hammersmith); *Afrobelhas Brazil* (British Council Tempo Festival); *Chocolate Cake* (Polka Theatre); *Hive City Legal* (The Roundhouse/ Hot Brown Honey); *Six Wives* and *The New Morning* (Theatre Royal Stratford East); *Bite Your Tongue* (Hackney Showroom/Talawa); *Blood Wedding*, *Romeo and Juliet and The Arsonists* (The Courtyard Theatre/CTTC); *Next Generation* (Zoonation); and *Cabin Fever* (Theatre503). Television credits include: *Frankenstein: How to Make a Monster* (BBC).

MOFETOLUWA AKANDE

Training: Bristol Old Vic Theatre School (winner of The Peter O'Toole Prize 2019). Theatre credits include: *A Christmas Carol* (Bristol Old Vic) and *Girls* (Theatre Royal Plymouth). Theatre whilst training: *The Life and Adventures of Nicholas Nickleby* (Bristol Old Vic); *We Want You to Watch* (Wardrobe Theatre); *Wonderboy* (Bristol Old Vic, Weston Studio); *Clybourne Park* (Bristol Old Vic, Weston Studio). Television/ radio credits include: *The Nevers* (HBO) and *The Secret Lives of Baba Segi's Wives* (BBC Radio 3).

KEZIAH JOSEPH

Keziah is an award-winning actress who has worked extensively in theatre and radio.

Theatre credits include: Olivier-nominated *Mr Gum and the Dancing Bear* (National Theatre); *The Lion, the Witch and the Wardrobe* (Bridge Theatre); Offie-winning *Language of Kindness* (UK tour). Broadcast credits include: *Crush Hour* (Amazon Audible); *The Archers* (BBC Radio 4); *Dr Who* (Big Finish); and *Octonauts* (Netflix).

AIMÉE POWELL

Credits include: *Nothello* (Belgrade Theatre, Coventry); *SeaView* (Belgrade Digital Media and Strictly Arts); *Sent to Cov* (Sky Arts); *This*

Little Relic (BBC Audio North); *Crongton Knights* (Pilot Theatre and Belgrade Theatre, Coventry); *Freeman* (Strictly Arts Theatre Company); *Doctors* (BBC One); *The Archers* (BBC Radio 4).

ALISTAIR HALL

Alistair is an actor and theatre maker from Chippenham. He graduated from RADA in 2019.

His debut solo show *Declan* received critical acclaim from the *Guardian*, *Attitude* magazine and more. On screen, he recently co-starred with Patricia Hodge in *Rose Pandemic.*

ACTORS TOURING COMPANY

Actors Touring Company (ATC) is a 'portable portal to the world'. We are a touring theatre company with an unrivalled track record in the commissioning, producing and touring of contemporary international plays.

Our work explores ideas of intersectionality, identity and belonging – opening up conversations across borders both geographic and cultural.

Since 1980, we've pioneered the touring of new global plays, often in world premiere translations of plays from Australia, Norway, Iran, Israel and the US – bringing global stories to audiences from Glasgow to Plymouth and Keswick to Ipswich.

ATC is currently developing projects with playwrights Nessah Muthy, Yasmin Joseph, writer/performer Ammar Haj Ahmad and partners Greenwich + Docklands International Festival, Soho Theatre and Theatre Royal Plymouth.

www.atctheatre.com

Signature productions include:

Family Tree by Mojisola Adebayo, commissioned by ATC and the Young Vic, premiered at the Greenwich + Docklands International Festival in August 2021. Winner of the 25th Alfred Fagon Award for Best New Play. Nationwide tour co-produced with Belgrade Theatre, Coventry in association with Brixton House, Spring 2023.

Tambo & Bones by Dave Harris, co-production with Theatre Royal Stratford East, June–July 2023 with national tour to follow in 2024.

Rice by Michele Lee, directed by Matthew Xia. Orange Tree Theatre, Autumn 2021 and 10-week nationwide tour, Spring 2022. Co-production with Orange Tree Theatre, toured in association with Theatre Royal Plymouth.

The Brothers Size by Tarell Alvin McCraney, directed by Bijan Sheibani, new revival of the ATC & Young Vic production planned for Broadway revival in 2024.

BELGRADE THEATRE is Coventry's largest professional theatre, producing and presenting a diverse range of shows, events and ground-breaking community and education initiatives. In its landmark building, across the region, the UK and online, it uses theatre to entertain, inspire, share the city's stories, uncover hidden histories, and unleash the creativity of diverse communities.

64 years ago, critic Kenneth Tynan saw the theatre's completion as the beginning of a new era. 'Enter most theatres and it's the gilded, cupidaceous past', he wrote. 'Enter this one, and you enter the future.' The Belgrade is in a period of transition into a new future, led by CEO Laura Elliot and Creative Director Corey Campbell. These leaders have ambitious plans to build on the Theatre's rich history of pioneering theatre, participation and talent development, to realize a lasting place of sanctuary for creatives and communities.

Through values of collaboration, evolution and authenticity, their working mission is to use the transformative power of theatre to enrich the people of Coventry and beyond.

Over the next three years, Laura Elliot and Corey Campbell will lead a people-first approach; prioritising co-creation and cultural democracy, aiming to be a leading example of a regional inclusive learning theatre that sits at the heart of its community.

BRIXTON HOUSE

Brixton House is a modern venue in the heart of Brixton, South London. Formerly Ovalhouse, the theatre has a long legacy of ground-breaking theatre and being a home for artists and a new generation of makers, artists, writers, producers, technicians and audiences, inspiring new experiences that develop community solidarity and passion for social change. Continuing its legacy of championing innovation and creative expression, Brixton House presents work that is rich in stories that resonate with its local, international and intergenerational communities. A place for people to come together, to create and enjoy performances, the venue houses two studio theatres, performance spaces, several rehearsal rooms and multi-use meeting rooms, as well as public spaces, a café and a bar. Brixton House is generously supported by London Borough of Lambeth, Arts Council England, Garfield Weston Foundation, The Wolfson Foundation, Cockayne Grants for the Arts, London Community Fund, The 29th May 1961 Charitable Trust.

ABOUT GREENWICH + DOCKLANDS INTERNATIONAL FESTIVAL (GDIF):

Produced by FESTIVAL.ORG, Greenwich + Docklands International Festival (GDIF) is London's free, annual outdoor theatre and performing arts festival. Taking place across Greenwich, Thamesmead and East London, GDIF is committed to co-creating, commissioning and presenting outdoor productions, which tell compelling stories in spectacular style, whilst bringing Londoners together.

During the pandemic GDIF delivered two exceptional editions of its annual festival of free, live outdoor arts. In the words of *Time Out* London, 'GDIF didn't just survive the last two years, it thrived in them'. GDIF forms part of the Royal Greenwich Festivals, and is the primary annual event produced by FESTIVAL.ORG.

Family Tree

Dedicated to Henrietta Lacks, Anarcha, Betsey, Lucy, the NHS workers who gave their lives during the Covid-19 pandemic and all the women, named and unnamed, who inspired this play

Characters

Four Black female performers play the following characters:

Henrietta Lacks, *inspired by the real African-American female, thirty-one in 1951.*

Three Black British National Health Service nurses, in their thirties, 2023, fictional, dead:

Ain (*also plays Anarcha*), *of Nigerian heritage.*
Bibi (*also plays Betsey*), *of African-Caribbean heritage.*
Lyn (*also plays Lucy*), *of mixed African-Caribbean and European heritage.*

Anarcha, **Betsey** *and* **Lucy**, *three enslaved African-American gynaecological patients/nurses, in their late teens/early twenties, inspired by real women in the 1840s.*
Oshun, *the Yoruba Orisha (deity) of sweet water, women, fertility and hairdressers, played by the actor who plays Ain/Anarcha.*
Smoking Man, *inspired by the 'Marlboro Man' from classic cigarette advertising. Played by a tall rugged white man in his thirties or forties with a strong physical presence.*
Tree, *the voice of a tree, multiple-layered, androgynous, Black tones. The voice could be recorded, live or both.*
Unnamed Black Women *perform various moving images throughout.*
Community Chorus: *where possible, a group of Black women also play Henrietta Lacks at the end of Scene Four into Scene Five. The chorus could also join at the end.*
Actor, *played by the actor playing Henrietta Lacks. A poetic urban griot (storyteller)/MC (master of ceremonies).*

Notes

- **Content:** readers, actors, makers and audiences may need to be made aware that this play deals with non-consensual medical experiments on Black women and children and cancer.
- **Casting:** a robust, total theatre, confident and low-ego, collaborative cast who are all emotionally, physically and politically brave, have a very strong sense of musicality in their textual delivery as well as the ability to sing or play music, with excellent physicality, vocal dexterity and power, generosity of spirit towards audiences and each other, is crucial. Ability to dress hair (or desire to learn) is a bonus!
- **Setting:** the play is set in a cemetery which is also a garden, both beautiful and eerie, sculptured but neglected. The play can be and has been performed both inside and outside.
- **Props and costumes:** these are indicated in the script.
- **Sustainability:** the production should be low waste with as light a carbon footprint as possible in all aspects including props, set, printing, travel, etc., otherwise the staging will contradict the content.
- **Accessibility**: access for D/deaf and disabled artists and audiences needs to be possible and integrated into the creative process from the inception, not as an afterthought.
- **Style:** this is not a realist play, it is magical but not sentimentally so; it is, sadly, a true horror. There is also *much* more joy to be found than is in words. It is also a ritual, funeral and celebratory feast.
- **Stage directions:** these are offers but not hard-and-fast instructions, unless there is an action that is crucial to following the narrative. Everything can be played with according to the vision of the creators and what works for the production.
- **Script:** amendments and cuts are at the discretion of the writer, unless otherwise indicated. Quotes from Toni

Morrison's *Beloved* (1987) are read aloud in the play by the character Bibi. Please have a copy of the novel available.

- **Music:** Black music of the African Diaspora, musicality and movement are integral. There is a lot more space for music, dance and movement than is indicated on the page. A series of physical images are indicated in the script, but more can be explored.
- **Some influential music:** 'Henrietta Our Hero' by Kamasi Washington, 'Mississippi Goddam' (live at Carneigie Hall) and 'Baltimore' by Nina Simone, 'Strange Fruit' by Billie Holiday, 'Black America' by Common featuring Stevie Wonder, 'My Power' by Nija, Beyoncé et al', 'D.N.A.' by Kendrick Lamar, 'The Israelites' by Desmond Dekker and more.
- **Some research books:** *Medical Apartheid* (2006) by Harriet A. Washington, *Medical Bondage* (2017) by Deirdre Cooper Owens, *The Immortal Life of Henrietta Lacks* (2010) by Rebecca Skloot, *Dying of Whiteness* (2019) by Jonathan M. Metzl, *The Hidden Life of Trees* by Peter Wohlleben (2017), *The Overstory* (2018) by Richard Powers, *Race and Nature* (2008) by Paul Outka, *Spillover* (2013) by David Quammen, *A History of the World in Seven Cheap Things* (2018) by Raj Patel and Jason W. Moore, *The Story of My Life* (1885) by J. Marion Sims, *The Holy Odu* (Yoruba scriptures pertaining to Oshun in particular), *And Still I Rise* (2006) by Doreen Lawrence, *Beloved* (1987) by Toni Morrison and more.

Prologue

Delivered by the **Actor** *who plays* **Henrietta** *at the entrance to the garden/cemetery. The* **Actor** *speaks in their own accent but they deliver the text in the role or persona of an MC/poetic urban griot.* **Actor** *changes into* **Henrietta** *whilst delivering the speech.* **Henrietta** *is imagined wearing a smart early 1950s ladies' skirt suit and blouse (as in the classic photo of her). The style of delivery has flavours of fast-paced reggae toasting, chatting, rapping, it is playful, rhythmic, sharp, intense and very quick, with exquisite clarity on every consonant, every vowel, vocal muscularity supported by deep breaths.*

Actor (*playing* **Henrietta**)   *Family Tree.* It's a play, a performance, a ritual, about human farming, farming humans, soil and the soul, seeds and cells, selling cells in prison cells prizing open, dividing, multiplying, multi-million incisions, incarcerations, extractions and experimentations – woman-child-man, in the lab, on the slab, in the land, the plantation womb and bred'ren bred for bread, planting and planning escape from living-dead, plotting from the plot to the pot but for the dread of night doctors, organ raiders, head drillers, cigarette smoking cowboys, cops with hands in pockets and the Klu Klux Klan; it's about cancer and capital, capitalism *as* cancer, cervical carcinoma in chicken culture (and the culture of chicken), compost and re-composition, giving of veins given in vain, philosophizing the threshold of Black pain, inhospitable hospitals, monitored monetary mortuaries, eugenic medical obscenities, Mississippi appendectomies and the bad blood between us at Tuskegee, not to mention sugar addiction affliction, disease dis-ease, fibroids, obesity, HIV, vitamin D deficiency, genes in jeans and cotton fields, cotton buds, cotton sheets and the unremembered history of gynaecology, implements' implications, dissecting dissections, fertilizing fertility slash secret sterilizations, speculums, scalpels, swabs of women slaves, taking us right up to today, coronavirus and giving-a-fuck-or-not about climate change. It's about shaking the plastic money tree and out-falling Covid-19 onto

a world that cannot breathe without change and cannot
breathe without trees, where a woman in some African
heaven hears her grown son calling 'Mama . . . Mama . . .'
. . . and she floats down . . . like leaves to the ground . . . lifts
his face from the dirt . . . and carries her baby home . . . no
more suffocation, pollution, asphyxiation . . . but the right to
cellular respiration. It's about the *original* 'extinction
rebellion' from the 'wretched of the earth', ethics of the
earth, risking the earth, dying of whiteness, dying to
whiteness to witness: burial as a form of gardening. See
three women come running loosening their plaits and
shaking their Afros free scattering seeds to sow soul food to
eat. (*We see three Black women running ecstatically fast then
stopping in a clearing, undoing their hair and shaking their heads
vigorously, scattering seeds on the ground.*) It's about where life
grows, where a woman breathes life into an inner floating
soul, drinking in, sustained in the Orisha of women, sweet
water and unlocked-down hairdressers. It's about finding a
route home through the roots of the tree they made on your
back, the tree you hung from, the tree of your lungs, the tree
in your womb, a family tree. It's about nursing the nursery,
curing creation, remedies and vaccinations against white
supremacist racism; birthing revolution, raising redemption,
finding yourself in the forest of futurity, the promise of
immortality and the matter of Black lives. Featuring:
Anarcha, Betsey and Lucy (the unremembered victim heroes
of plantation gynaecology at the hands Dr Sims – pulled
down from his plinth); starring: three NHS nurses – Ain,
Bibi and Lyn, calling on the names of Doreen Lawrence and
Fannie Lou Hamer, vibing with Beyoncé and bowing to the
wisdom of Toni Morrison. Oh and there's a cameo by the
Man from Marlboro and in the leading role the everlasting
Henrietta Lacks. Rest in peace! Rise in peace! Rise in Power!

Scene One – Henrietta waves

Henrietta *is awoken at the edge of the cemetery/garden. She is a warm and generous-spirited, charismatic, feminine and feisty, small-statured and strong-minded thirty-one-year-old African-American woman; born and raised in rural Virginia on a tobacco share-cropping plantation, she moved with her husband, Day, to Baltimore, Maryland. In her earth life, the real* **Henrietta** *was known to be very sociable, loved to laugh, family and community-loving, generous, caring, fun, a great cook, had an open door, loved music, dancing, partying with friends – and in this play, still does! Since her death seventy years ago, making her now over a hundred years old, she has been observing and learning. However, right now, she has no idea where her spirit has landed or why. She builds a direct relationship with the audience from the start. They are with her wherever she is. As if waking from a dream,* **Henrietta** *waves lovingly and longingly to her husband, Day, whom only she sees in the distance.*

Henrietta (*calling and waving*)   Day! Day! . . .

(*In deepest sorrow, to herself.*) Oh no . . .

I didn't make it . . .

I'm so sorry . . .

(*Calling.*) Take good care of our babies' Day

Go visit Elsie

I love you!

I'll watch over you!

(*To the audience.*) Look now,

They're laying me in the ground

(*Sensing the weather.*) Thunder! Storm coming!

(*Calling.*) Get the children out of the rain, Day!

Make sure you all have something hot to eat!

Don't worry about me, I'm fine

Pain is all gone

Can't feel a thing

Except love

And sorrow

Bye, bye, babies . . . bye, bye.

She waves goodbye. **Smoking Man**, *who has been watching since the start, strikes a match and lights up a cigarette.* **Henrietta** *looks and addresses her first question to* **Smoking Man**, *who observes this and all scenes. Potential entry and exit points are suggested.* **Smoking Man** *grows weaker and sicker as the play progresses.*

Henrietta (*to* **Smoking Man**)   Do you ever picture your own funeral?

I see it again and again

And I feel more and more

I am repeating myself

That myself is repeating . . .

(*Studying the sky, to the audience.*) Can you see faces? . . .

I see clouds

Of white coats

And white faces

A sky of blue eyes

Watery gazes

Mouths agape

In amazement

I feel myself

I feel *my-selves*

Floating back

On cool pools of glass

A myriad of bright lights

Shoot through all of me's

Like sharp rays of the sun

(*Smelling.*) And I swear I can smell . . .

(*Sniff.*) Chicken?

I hear voices

Incessantly

Talking

About *me* . . .

Marking me out

Not like the white boys' stones and slurs when I was a little girl on my way to school

No

These voices sound . . .

In awe

(*Shifting her voice to scientists whom she hears in her head.*)

'Astounding'

'Phenomenal'

'Remarkable'

Saying my name, over and over:

'Henrietta Lacks

Coloured woman,

Mother,

Tobacco farmer,

Age: Thirty-one

Year: 1951

Johns Hopkins Hospital

Baltimore, Maryland

Cervical cancer

Treated

But died

Dark purple tumour

Removed from womb

Observe this

Petri dish.

Astonishing.

Her cells continue to divide

Multiply

She has,

In a sense,

Outlived her own life

Hers, the only cells to survive

Thrive

Outside . . .'

(*Her own voice.*) Outside?

(*Scientist's voice again.*) 'The boundaries of the human body'

Am I *alive*?

'Henrietta:

He.

Lacks:

La.

'HeLa''

Healer?

It appears

I am a wonder.

Image – Smoking Man carries a Black woman on his back

Music. **Smoking Man** *is seen by the audience (but not* **Henrietta***), walking, carrying a limp* **Black Woman** *across his back.*

Scene Two – Deeper in

Henrietta *moves deeper into the garden/cemetery, trying to figure out where she is, what is this dreamlike, eerie place?*

Henrietta   Where on earth am I?

It's too lonely for heaven

And too peaceful for hell . . .

'Sell! Sell! Cells!'

It's all they talk about

(*Hearing another scientist in her head.*) 'The tiniest seed of life

Divides

In the womb

Two by two

Daughter cells

From the mother cell

And inside each cell

Genes

And inside your genes

Your DNA'

DNA?

Did. Not. Ask?

Did not tell!

They took cancer cells from my cervix

Yes

Swished me in *chicken* culture

That's that smell!

And did not ask

And did not tell

I am a stolen miracle

Well . . .

Scene Three – Ain, Bibi and Lyn, chat, plait and question

Ain, **Bibi** and **Lyn** *appear, walking and talking through another part of the cemetery/garden, as if starting their tea break, carrying mugs and hair products including water-based moisturizing spray.* **Bibi** *has forgotten that she is dead. Their dialogue is upbeat, pacy, punchy and precise, sharp on cues, no pauses unless stated. They do not address or see the audience.* **Smoking Man** *appears in the scene, watching, smoking.*

Ain   2 per cent Neanderthal.

Lyn   What?

Ain   Europeans. 2 per cent Neanderthal.

Lyn   Here we go.

Ain   Just sayin. Fact.

Bibi   I read that (*i.e. I read that too*).

Lyn   Racist.

Ain   I'm not saying they're inferior

Lyn   Racist, plain and simple.

Bibi   Maybe the 2 per cent is their racism gene. Maybe they can't help it.

Lyn   Not exactly helpful is it?

Ain   It is to me! All that time they treated us like we were another species when all along it was –

Bibi   Them.

Ain   Exactly!

Lyn   What if you're both? What are you saying about my mum? What are you saying about *me*?

Bibi   1 per cent?

Lyn   Fuck off.

Bibi (*teasing*)   Aww it's only a 'ickle bit

Lyn   Have you seen your batty?

Bibi   What?

Lyn   Have you taken a good look at your own batty lately?

Bibi   What you saying?

Lyn   It is flat, Bibi. *Flat*. And it ain't from lying on the slab.

Bibi   Slab?

Lyn *swiftly turns* **Bibi** *around and gestures to her bum.*

Lyn   I could iron my scrubs on that.

Ain   You didn't!

She cracks up laughing loudly.

Bibi   Well, you can fuck off, your grandad was PORTUGUESE!

Ain *is mortified at the revelation of this secret!*

Bibi   All this time I never knew there was a Lagos in the Algarve . . .

Ain *could cry inside.*

Bibi   Neanderthal, my arse (*or ta' rass*).

Lyn   Literally.

They position themselves to work on each other's hair/heads at three levels, e.g. one on the ground, another seated on a gravestone above her and another standing. **Bibi** *works on* **Ain**'*s hair.* **Ain** *works on* **Lyn**'*s. Oiling, massaging, combing/braiding/twisting – whatever is desired.* **Lyn** *pulls up and plays with matter on the ground.*

Ain   I wasn't trying to be provocative. (*Sadness behind the sarcasm.*) I have simply decided to use my sudden and unexpected 'spare time' –

Bibi   What you on about?

Ain   My 'spiritual sabbatical', my –

Lyn   – early retirement.

Ain   That's it! I've decided to use my 'infinite early retirement' to do my own personal research project on 'why people'.

Lyn   You mean white people?

Ain   I said what I mean. Why people:

Why do they re-write history?

Why do they delete history?

Why can't they take criticism?

Why can't they cope with their guilt?

Why are they so fragile?

Why do they make everything about them?

Why can't they imagine themselves in our shoes?

Why do they think they are the centre of the world?

Why do they run the world?

Why do they believe they've got the divine right to rule? Us. Our jewels. Their crown.

Why?

Why did they colonize us, enslave us, keep killing us, or just watch us die?

Why do they always want to make some *banal* comparison when you talk about racism?

Why do they expect us to shine their medals when they go on *one* Black Lives Matter demonstration? Or read a Black book? Or go out with a Black man?

Why do they wanna display us as their *one* Black friend?

Why are they so self-satisfied?

Why the sense of entitlement?

Why don't they stand up and fight when we aren't treated right?

Why don't they care when we disproportionately die?

Why people.

Why?

Beat.

Bibi   This must be the longest tea break ever.

*They **All** take a deep breath together. Then continue on the hair/heads.*

Lyn   I get what you're saying, Ain, but there's also a lot of white people –

Ain   *why* people –

Lyn   – *people* trying to make a difference.

Ain   Like who?

Lyn   Some of our colleagues for a start.

Ain   None of them have got any power! Name me one person in a position of *power*.

Pause while **All** *try hard to think of someone; it's a guessing game.*

Lyn   Joe Biden!

Ain   Gimme a break. He only won cos of Kamala Harris.

Bibi   She is so sexy.

Ain   Plus Biden's Irish and they used to be Black.

Lyn   Huh?

Bibi   I literally can't think of anyone.

Pause while **All** *think hard.*

Bibi   Prince Harry?

All *laugh hard and brief.* **Lyn** *punctuates with her line.*

Lyn   Greta Thunberg.

Ain   Fuck Greta Thunberg.

Lyn   Ain!

Ain   Fuck her and fuck climate change.

Lyn   You can't say that.

Ain   Just did. Felt GREAT!

Lyn   Climate change is bigger than Covid.

Ain   So why should I give a shit now?! Let it change! *Why* people started the fire, let *why* people put it out.

Lyn   Jesus you're so bitter. She's only a child.

Bibi   You can't say she's not making a difference.

Ain   Day off school – how is that making a difference?

Bibi   I'd love a day off.

Lyn (*a little irritated*)   Well, you can have as many as you like now can't you, Bibi.

Bibi   Ohhhh . . . (*i.e I get it. Now with clarity, as if on a picket line.*) We're on strike! Lyn?

A deep breath, then continue working on each other's heads.
Smoking Man *exits, coughing.*

Ain   Skinny Swedish kid gets upset and the whole world sits up. But it takes kneeling for ten minutes on a Black man's neck for them to even notice they been riding on our backs for centuries. And I am not just talking about the men, because a lot of them admit it. But *why* women, they got away with it and they're getting away with it – still. And as soon as you say anything it's: (**Ain** *takes the water spray and spurts from her eyes impersonating crying, it should be funny.*) I swear sea levels rising ain't nothing to do with air pollution, it's all the why women that keep crying when you try and address their racism. I mean does Greta Thurnberg even exist?

Lyn   Of course she exists!

Ain   How do you know?

Bibi   Come on, Ain, she's all over the papers.

Ain   So that's how you know she exists? We are definitely dead then.

Bibi   What?

Ain (*ignoring the heart of* **Bibi**'s *question*)   Didn't you see the papers in the pandemic? 'Clapping for carers'. And whose faces were on the front pages? Boris and a bunch a why women.

She does a quick impression of Boris Johnson on the front page, mumbling some inane crap along the lines of 'definitely not a party, no, no, no, thems the breaks'.

I didn't see your faces so looks like you don't exist.

Lyn   They could have named it the Seacole instead of the Nightingale Hospital. Walk into any clinic in this country – it can't function without people of colour.

Ain   Ain't all people got colour?

Lyn   You know what I mean.

Ain   No. I do not. Like it. P.O.C. B.A.M.E. All just another way of making 'white' normal. Plus, even woke Greeks are getting brownie points these days, calling themselves 'people of colour' when it suits them. You know what Anna said to me when she got promoted and none of us even got asked to apply?

Bibi   'I wanted to be an ally but I had to think of my kids.'

Lyn   Ally?!

Ain   A-lie! (*Play on ally.*)

Bibi   And who babysat those kids?!

Lyn   Jeez, who needs enemies when you've got 'allies'.

Ain   *Traitors*! When they wanna be *traitors* to whyness, *then* we can talk

Bibi (*punctuating* **Ain***'s line*)   seen.

Ain   You can't call me racist, Lyn. It was never about DNA or the melanin. It was always and only ever is about the *money*. And if I'd have got that promotion, I wouldn't be sitting here for eternity twisting your hair.

Bibi   What do you mean?

Ain   I would have been higher up food chain and I wouldn't have beeeen EATEN!

Scene Four – Henrietta's story

Henrietta *gets comfortable, paints her fingernails red and intimately recounts her story.*

Henrietta   It was an ordinary day in an ordinary life

But sometimes it seems Black folks don't get the right to be ordinary.

Might be just waiting for a bus, sitting on the couch, leaving a store, driving along . . .

Then something extraordinary always seems bound to happen.

Anyways, it was an ordinary day and there was me

Great-great-grand-daughter of a slave named 'Mourning'

(As in grief, not the opposite of night)

Who grew up to marry a man we called 'Day'

(As in light)

Whose ancestor was owned by a tobacco slaver name of 'Lacks'

(As in, what was it that he *did not* have?)

This Mrs Henrietta Lacks,

Mother of five,

Sees (*seeing them in the moment*) little red spots

Feels a deep tight knot

And knows (*telling herself*) I have to be brave.

(*Getting up and re-embodying the memory described, keeping it all live.*)

So here I am, walking down the hospital corridor

On my way to the 'coloured ward'

I stop and touch Jesus' white stone feet

Pray not to picture what's beneath *my* feet

Deep in the basement.

We all knew about it

How they kept pieces of our people down there.

Common prayer was 'Lord, if I die, let it be in summer'[1]

When it was too hot to store all the cadavers

But in the chill of winter the 'night doctors' would take a cut of all they could profit

Livers, lungs, hearts, all kinds of body parts

From the dead and the living as well

Scared us to hell,

Men in white coats

And white hoods

On horses

Burning crosses

Hospital sheets

With cut-out holes,

Living ghosts.

And on that ordinary day Dr Howard Jones

Opens me up with a cold speculum

Peers into the most private part of me.

(*As if it is happening now.*) I hold my breath, eat the pain

While they set a fire of radium inside me

---

[1] Paraphrased from Harriet Washington, *Medical Apartheid: The Dark History of Medical Experimentation on Black Americans from Colonial Times to the Present* (New York: Anchor Books, 2008), p. 131.

Trying to burn that cancer out of my body.

I wave to Day and the children from my window.

So lonely,

Like I was in prison,

And inside millions of locked cells

With no one to watch over me

(*A surgeon.*) 'She is covered in tumors that look like pearls.'

Pearls from the penitentiary, my babies' legacy

There's a whole lot of money in a mortuary.

What made them think that was all right?

What kept them all silent?

Why the long quiet?

Quiet as death out here too.

What is this place?

Where is the music?!

Music plays, something upbeat and very now. **Henrietta** *shouting over the music, asks an audience member . . .*

What year are we in? Hm?

She pursues the question, e.g. 'I said what year is this?'

(*Repeating an audience member's answer.*) 2023?!

That makes meeee . . .

One hundred and change years YOUNG! (*Laughing.*)

Let's get some drinks flowing then, where's the food?!

Don't the dead deserve a party?!

Especially when they're still alive!

She laughs and dances exuberantly celebrating her miraculous existence. During the dance, another **Black Woman***, dressed exactly like* **Henrietta***, runs and joins in dancing, then another* **Black Woman** *and another – as many as possible – the* **Community Chorus** *are like multiplying cells.*

Scene Five – Ain, Bibi and Lyn chill, plait and read

Ain*,* **Bibi** *and* **Lyn** *sit in the same place as before but they have swapped positions. Quiet after the storm/morning after feeling.* **Lyn** *works on* **Ain***'s head who works on* **Bibi** *whilst* **Bibi** *reads. Just being and breathing gently but perceptibly, until* **Lyn** *breaks the silence.*

Lyn   What you reading?

Bibi   The Bible.

Ain   Bit late for that, sis.

Bibi   Never too late. (*A beat.*) It's Toni Morrison really.

Lyn   Oooh which one?

Bibi   *Beloved.* Been eating books lately.

Pause. **Bibi** *reads on.*

Lyn   Give us a bit.

Bibi *flicks through Toni Morrison's* Beloved, *finds her favourite section and reads through it.*[2]

Closes the book. **All** *breathe.*

---

[2] Excerpt from Toni Morrison's *Beloved* (London: Vintage Books, [1987] 2007), pp. 102–3: 'When warm weather came . . . her great big heart.'.

Scene Six – Henrietta on cancer

Straight in with speech, still dancing lightly, now with a drink in hand, **Henrietta** *is upbeat, playful with rhythms and tones, maybe singing, pulsating forward.*

Henrietta   So, what exactly *is* cancer?

Cancer is like . . .

Shopping malls and plastic toys

Colonizing cowboys

Spreading, taking over, claiming the land

Forest fire and flood.

Cancer is a bank

Feeding on debts and dreams

A property investor taking over your house, gentrifying your street

The fat bankrupt billionaire who still wants more meat in his cheeseburger

The expanding Klu Klux Klan or a royal family

Breed, marry, breed, marry, reign, reign, reign

Match, kindle, wood, cross, flame, flame, flame

And hear me now, it does not want to stop

It presses in on everything – that's the pain part

And cancer is a *liar*

Only hurts *after* it's started trying to destroy ya

The pain is delayed

(*Beat.*)

Like trauma.

And it never stops wanting growth

Well, somebody has got to say – ENOUGH

Someone's gotta stop it

Someone's gotta take a scalpel to it

Someone's gotta cut it out and say:

FUCK CANCER! FUCK THE BANKS, THE BANKRUPT
BILLIONAIRES, LANDOWNERS, SLAVE OWNERS,
BORDER CONTROLLERS. FUCK COLUMBUS,
CRUSADERS AND COLONIZERS, OCCUPIERS,
COWBOY DEBT COLLECTORS, COMPANY
DIRECTORS, CAPITALIST COMMANDERS OF ALL
THEIR EMPIRES. FUCK THE BIG C, THE LITTLE C,
FUCK ALL OF YOUR CELLS!

I am sorry for cursing (*real sorrow*)

but premature death,

makes you really upset.

(*Breathing, composing herself.*)

But here comes the good part:

I had a super cancer

A purple super cancer

A cancer supernova

A cancer superpower (*repeating like a jazz refrain*)

A purple super-cancer

A cancer supernova

A cancer superpower

So that means:

Whilst my corpse seeps into the Baltimore soil

My cancer cells don't even need my body anymore

And that's why they could one day use my cells

To find a cure for cancer *itself*

And THAT is a *beautiful* thing!

And I say that should be free

For you, for me for all the human family

Freeeeeeeeeeeeeeee!

Except, somebody has been making MILLIONS out of ME!

(*Knocks back her drink.*)

And I didn't get any CREDIT

While my family got into DEBT

And couldn't afford health care!

They could have all had a much better life from my body

But they never knew the truth from the newspapers because the doctors re-named me Helen Larson and Helen Lane!

White women's names!

Took a white woman called Skloot to lead my children to the root of the story

And I am grateful for that

But no one actually asked me how I *feel*.

(*Answering her own question.*) I am a farm!

We were their harvest!

And they reap what they did not sow!

Reaping and raping and reaping and raping,

stealing and slicing and stitching us up

When does it STOP?!

Wasn't it enough that we farmed their tobacco

Turning our fingers yellow?

I spent every spare cent on nail polish

And I don't even smoke!

What kind of people burn something that doesn't warm you?

Numbs the hunger but doesn't feed you?

Probably ends up killing you

What for, just so you can see yourself breathe?

Brought us all the way from Africa for that?!

But I don't want y'all to think I'm some kind of victim

Hell, HeLa didn't make it easy for the medicine men

We added what you might call a complication

(*Loving playing this out.*) In the shape of one almighty migration

My stolen cells spread like weeds in a flower bed

But weeds are just plants at the wrong time in the wrong place

Everything gardens, everything's got a purpose[3]

Mine makes their lives just a little more difficult:

Moving through laboratory test tubes from Maryland to Moscow (*rhyme = cow/pow*)

My cells are so POWERFUL

They've got the Midas touch! (*This could be sung, like the tune by Midnight Star.*)

Everything I touch turns to LACKS

And that's how it came out I was in fact: BLACK!

(*Keep it in the present moment.*) Oooooooh they got a problem,

---

[3] Thank you to Asmelash Dagne for this line, permaculture workshop, Prinzessinnen Garten, Berlin, July 2019.

They gotta decipher this cell from that, the white from the Black

So what do they do?

Take DNA from my children and LIE about why they're doing it too!

But in the process a researcher lets it slip to my sister-in-law

That (*as a Black researcher*) 'she has given rise to the greatest biological findings in history!'

And why do you think it is that most of you have never even heard of me? Hm?

Goodbye, Helen Larson, farewell Helen Lane!

Presenting HENRIETTA LACKS!

Go on and fish me out of the net with your *cell phone*

(*Encouraging them to take phones out.*) Go on . . .

(*To an audience member.*) Try 'buy HeLa cell line'

Three hundred and sixty-seven US dollars for a *vial* (*sounds like 'vile'*)

There's even a manual for how to use me

(*In disgust.*) Do-it-yourself.

Well, I refuse to be owned by anybody

I belong to GOD and me and everybody is everybody

And everything is . . .

(*Prompt the audience to respond.*) I said everybody is everybody and everything is?

Audience   Everything!

Henrietta   And everyplace is everywhere

But WHERE?

(*She sees a picnic hamper of food.*)

Food, at last, YEAH!

(*To audience members, gently, whilst sharing fruit with them.*)

Do you know anyone who had leukaemia?

Haemophilia? Parkinson's disease? HIV? . . .

Well, they got treatments through my cells, through *me*.

(*Playfully to one male presenting audience member.*) And you've either had the flu or herpes – am I right?

You don't need to disclose

Just know you got better – because of me!

HeLa helped develop chemotherapy, cloning, gene mapping

What we know about chromosomes and disability,

Artificial intelligence – starts with me!

And all those beautiful IVF babies wouldn't have been born without me!

And they'll never get polio after HeLa put an end to *that* pandemic

(*Like a superhero.*) And now I'm on the frontline fighting Covid-19!

But they're even buying up that vaccine!

Greed!

What about *my* people?

What about *our* children?

What about Elsie?!

She suddenly bursts into tears and runs away. No one saw this coming.

Scene Seven – Ain, Bibi and Lyn chat, plait and chicken

Lyn *now works on* **Bibi***'s hair,* **Bibi** *works on* **Ain**. **Lyn** *is very tense.* **All** *take a deep breath together, then:*

Lyn   I'm hungry. I fancy a big bargain bucket of chicken.

Ain (*genuine*)   Wow.

Lyn (*pulsating forward with hunger/anger*)   I want it bad. I want it fake. In a cardboard box. Nothing organic. I don't even want the kind of chicken that's seen a cage. I want a petri-dish chicken. Test-tube chicken. Genetically modified never even seen daylight so white its transparent and I can see right through to the bone. Grown without feathers so they don't have to slow down the process with plucking. So young it ain't even clucking. Pumped full of hormones, deep fried in an oil disaster and battered in sugar from exploitation island. Gimme that slave-trade dinner. Gimme that addiction bitchin' chicken chucked at the school's-out chubby chubby chicken children. Gimme that finger-licking stereotyping feel-good cheapie cheapie chicken. I wanna chomp n' chew through that delectable diabetes obesity dirty birdie while I'm sitting at the back of bus, clogging up my arteries with more cholesterol than there are cars stuck in traffic on the New Cross Road. (*Or insert a local hellishly busy polluted road.*) Bring me that finger-fucking good nasty tasty ass white chicken NOW. (*Beat.*) Two breasts and a leg.

Bibi   And a milkshake.

Ain   Not a vegan anymore then?

Lyn   I was never vegan. I was Ital. Like my grandad. I don't care anymore.

Bibi   Cigarette after?

Lyn   Yeah go on then.

Ain   Sucking on a white man's cock.

Lyn   Eh?

Ain   That's what they used to say, back in the day, smoking a cigarette is sucking on a white man's cock.

Lyn   Yeah. I'll suck it so hard it disappears into thin air . . .

All *breathe deeply.* **Smoking Man** *appears.*

Lyn   I'll never understand it. I put my life on the line. I'm taking blood from this old codger who looks like he's done his best to kill himself with Special Brew his whole life but do I judge him? I just gotta do it, gently as I can and he starts coughing and shouting, 'I wanna English nurse! Get this fucking coon offa me! I demand my rights!' And not one of those fuckers, not *one* of them says anything . . . and when I talked to Becky about it she said 'I thought you were more thick-skinned' and pulls, like this. (*Pulling her own skin on her hand, visibly upset.*)

Bibi   You OK, babe?

Lyn   Yeah it's just . . . still so upsetting. Even now.

Bibi   I know. I'm third-generation NHS and they couldn't even make sure I had the right size PPE. Sewed it myself.

Ain   You're too good, Bibi. I go Tesco's in my oversize scrubs, brat spits at me, calls me a superspreader and they treat me like *I've* done something to provoke it.

Lyn   Angry Black woman: 'Call security!'

Bibi (*understated, calm*)   I'm not angry – I'm furious.

Lyn   And they think they understand prejudice because: 'I've actually been on Unconscious Bias Training.'

Ain   How can you be unconscious for four hundred years?!

Lyn   About to find out . . .

Bibi   Don't say that.

Lyn   It's true!

Bibi   What are you on about?

Lyn (*a flash of frustration*)   We keep telling you, Bibi!

All *breathe*.

Bibi   Am I . . . sleeping?

Ain   Kinda . . .

Bibi (*sadly searching her memory*)   I was so tired . . . I should have taken the day off but . . . I had the surgery during my lunch break. That bitch is pulling at my polyp for *ten minutes*. And I'm breathing through it, going on about gynaecology, how it all started during slavery, experiments on Black women and she's just pretending not to hear. Then eventually nursey pokes her mousey head up over my fanny, looks at me like I farted in her face and says 'cotton'.

Lyn   Cotton?

Bibi   Bit of tampon. Then she goes back in and yanks. But I go straight back down to work. Bleed. Anaemic. Knackered. On my feet twenty hours between the kids and the wards but I'm not letting anyone call me lazy. I even feel guilty now.

Lyn   Mad, innit?

Bibi   I was so so tired . . .

Lyn   Do you think that's why you fell down?

Bibi   I fell down? . . .

Pause. Breathe.

Bibi   I can't remember. I'd just put the kids to bed, I was running a bath and . . . next thing . . . I feel . . . wood.

She is resisting being overwhelmed in sadness until **Ain** *breaks the moment.*

Ain   You heard the one about tampons and why women?

Lyn   DON'T.

Ain   Both stuck-up cunts.[4]

Lyn   Ain!

Ain   Black women die in childbirth *five times* more than why women – they ignore our pain! And if you got polyps or fibroids or just heavy periods they can't wait to whip out the whole shop!

Bibi   Anything to stop us breeding. Ironic, seeing as that's why they stole us in the first place.

Ain   And when they wanna cure an STD the first people they wanna try the drug out on is us. Or pretend to be curing us from syphilis when they're really just watching how we die.

Bibi   Tuskegee . . .

Ain   Makes me sick. And they're surprised when our people don't trust the vaccine.

Beat.

Bibi   You lot having it?

Lyn (*now losing her temper*)   There's no point now is there?!

Bibi*'s memory loss/denial is now unbearable for* **Lyn** *who is also processing loss.*

Bibi   Sorry. Lyn. Tell me again.

Lyn (*softer*)   We're dead, sis. Dead.

Breathe but **Ain** *breaks it.*

Ain (*upbeat, fake joy*)   Like the Queen!

Bibi (*feigning shock*)   Beyoncé died?![5] (**Lyn** *in disbelief at* **Bibi**.) I know. 'The' Queen.

---

[4] I heard a version of this joke in the play *Clybourne Park* back in 2011. Thanks to the author, Bruce Norris.
[5] Thank you, Vaginal Davis.

Ain   Only real difference between us is she was a born billionairess who passed peacefully in a palace at ninety-six and – WHAT A SEND-OFF!

Lyn (*sharp in, correcting*)   It was a castle and you can't say she didn't work hard.

Ain   She didn't work hard – said it! (*Giving a royal wave like it's really hard work.*)

Lyn *going to tell* **Ain** *off but* **Bibi** *is sharp in with:*

Bibi   WE ALL WORKED HARD. We all worked hard. We didn't deserve this!

Beat, of agreement, acknowledging their shared loss.

Ain   There's not a one of them I truss. Not one – truss.

Lyn   Not even my mum.

Ain *and* **Bibi** *look at her. A big revelation.*

Lyn   Not even my mum. (**Lyn** *has never told anyone this.*) When I told her, just before I got Covid, that I thought Jerome was 'the one' all she said was, 'I could never imagine having Black grandchildren'. I said, 'What, what about me?' And she just carried on polishing the cutlery. She could go out with a Black man, have a cute little caramel baby with him but . . . having a child that comes from her line and is as dark as him . . . now that repulses her, she can't even *imagine* it. Good job it'll never happen now.

Breathe.

Bibi   Why do they hate us?

Ain   The *million dollar* question.

Scene Eight – Elsie

Henrietta *sings to* **Elsie**, *drawing the audience in, gently.*

Henrietta
    Hush, little baby don't say a word
    Mama's gonna buy you a mockingbird

And if that mockingbird don't sing
Mama's gonna buy you . . . (*inventing a lyric*) pearls
on a string
And if those pearls are made of stone
Mama's gonna bring you right on home . . .

(*Humming.*)

My sweet little Elsie

Had epilepsy

And was deaf

They said she was simple

And it was best

To send her away for care

To a hospital named Crownsville

I always went to visit

Even after I died.

And that's when I saw what I can never un-see:

(*Seeing it all in the moment.*) They're opening up my baby's crown, drilling a hole

And I am screaming from my soul, 'NO NO NO!

You can't do that to my baby, you can't do that to a CHILD!'

Breathe into her brain? So you can look inside and see what epilepsy is instead of asking her how it feels!

(*Like a Black Lives Matter funeral sermon, music maybe.*)

And I hear Elsie calling, 'Mama, Mama . . .'

Like George Floyd was calling

Like Sandra Bland was calling

Like Stephen Lawrence was calling

'Mama, Mama . . .'

And who else?

Who else was calling? . . . Say their names?

(*Perhaps audience members will say names until . . .*)

(*To* **Elsie**.) I'm so sorry, baby . . .

They didn't do experiments for our children

But to find cures for theirs!

Not for Elsie!

But for some white woman's disabled child

And they wanna keep the healing for themselves

When the health of the people belongs to all of the people!

Amen?

(*Some audience members might respond with Amen – let this happen.*)

Here's a deal:

If you can create a vaccine for racism,

Find a cure for white supremacy,

An immunization for discrimination for all of your children

You can have my permission

You can take my cells!

And my eyes and my ears and my tongue and my lungs

Have it all!

For free!

What do you say?

Devil?

Deal?

(*She has gone too far, spooked herself.*) Ohhhhhhhhhh, Henrietta . . . you better be careful when you make a deal with the devil in a garden, you never know where it might end.

Scene Nine – Making a remedy

Anarcha *and* **Betsey** *walk through, gathering herbs in the garden. They then grind the herbs, perhaps in a huge mortar, like pounding yam.*

Lucy   Anarcha, do you think they mean to eat us?

Startled, **Anarcha** *and* **Betsey** *stop foraging herbs and look at each other, wordless. Then continue with the action, into grinding the herbs.*

Lucy   My great-grandmother said that's what they feared most . . . when they was stolen. That's why the stealers looked so pale and sickly, that's why they seemed so hateful and angry, that it must be because they were so very, very . . . hungry . . . What other need would be so great that people would do such a thing, they must be so *desperate* that they crossed the great expanse of water and hunted us deep into the forest. But some fought fiercely and refused to be food and some chose the waves and some got fed to sharks and some . . . somehow . . . survived. Like my great-grandmother. Survived but still fearing that . . . because they can't seem to grow without us, toil without us, harvest without us, sex without us, birth without us, nurse without us, raise children without us, clean without us, cook without us, dance without us, feel good about themselves without one of us close that maybe one day they won't be able to survive without us at all and so they'll do what they first came for, they'll open up their mouths and push us down inside their throats and fill their bellies and that will be the end of us: an eaten people. Extinct. Shat. Into the soil.

Betsey   What is this talk, Lucy?

Lucy   I was shining the cutlery and staring so hard at my reflection in a spoon that I didn't notice when Dr Sims came in, took it out of my hand and I swear, Betsey, he licked his lips.

Betsey   That's just a tick.

Lucy   He licked his lips! And everybody knows Dr Sims bought himself a shoe-repair kit from the cobbler and opened up the newborn babies' heads like pomegranates. Everybody knows. They lynch runaways and roast them and cut them up into tiny pieces for sale. I saw teeth strung on a necklace on a store in town. Don't you think it's possible? Betsey?

Betsey   That he wants us for soup?

Lucy   *Yes*.

Betsey   No. He doesn't fatten us enough for that.

Grinding the herbs they have picked.

Lucy   Bones. There's a lot in a bone. He wants to suck out my marrow. I'll rub my arms and legs with chilli pepper.

Anarcha   Don't you think Dr Sims could have feasted on me and Betsey years ago if that's what they wanted? Sims needs us so he can change the fate Satan gave Eve back in the garden. Starting with a fistula.

Betsey   And ending with a fist-full-a dollars, (*quoting Sims*) 'Control the womb, control the world! This will be my finest hour . . .' He'll be tending ladies from here to England . . . If he can get the method right.

Anarcha   He made the speculum out of two silver spoons, Lucy.

Betsey   No slavery without babies. That's why he's stopped breaking their heads.

Lucy   How do you know?

Betsey   I hear him practise his lectures, convincing his wife that it's not that 'I like having my head between Black legs, the smell repels me but I am destined for this'. But Mrs Sims is suspicious. Why does he spend all his time trying to put our broken bowls back together and barely touches her porcelain skin? Behind every white man is a white woman staring.

Anarcha   It has nothing to do with wanting to eat you and me and Betsey. We're meant for the plantation, not the plate.

Betsey   The plot not the pot.

Anarcha   But if we are lucky, if we can endure the surgery, we might, one day, get healed.

Lucy   He might fix me but he can never heal me. Only you two know how to do that.

Scene Ten – Eden?

Henrietta *grounds herself beneath a huge tree.* **Smoking Man** *looks on.*

Henrietta   If that old serpent would have come to me, instead of Eve

And said, (*playing Satan, posh English perhaps*) 'Go on, take from that tree',

I would have said: 'No.

Just because it grows, does not mean I have to have it.

Just because it's there, does not mean I need to take it.'

I would have said: 'Adam, honey, let's just stick to being naked, not having to work and painless childbirth, he can keep that apple of power-knowledge, I'll go suck on a mango instead.'

That's what I would have said

If this was Eden.

(*Struck by the possibility of a big revelation of who and where she is.*)

If this is . . .? And I am? . . .

(*Breathing deeply at the thought.*)

Before anyone cries, 'Blasphemy'

Hear me out, patiently

I'm just *speculating*

From my little petri dish

Allow me this:

What *if*

This *is* some kind of Eden or Kingdom

And I have been chosen by (*points upwards*)

If the Lord would choose a Jew for a son,

(*Daring herself to imagine.*) Why not a Black daughter?

Brown-eyed Messiahs . . .

Carpenter / Mother

Turn the tables / Lay the tables

Feed the five thousand / Feed the family

Walk on water / Break waters

Raise the dead / Raise the children

Disciples and descendants, miracles and cures . . .

At thirty-three and thirty-one.

The kiss of Judas and the scalpel of a surgeon

Peter denied / Doctors lied

A crown of thorns / The 'coloured' ward

Splayed on a crucifx / Cancer of the cervix . . .

Mother Mary weeps at his feet / Daddy Day cries kids to sleep

Take his body down, lay him in the tomb

Cut out pieces from my womb

Anoint him with oils, roll the rock before the door

Lock me in the coloured freezer, behind the law

Three days in the garden, like the sun, see him rise!

Microscope and light, I start to divide

(*In genuine praise.*) Behold, our Saviour the LORD, Jesus Christ!

(*More internal again, this is risky thinking.*) From the slab to the lab to the jab

And still I multiply . . .

And they look to Him, and to me?

For some kind of healing.

Now don't get it twisted

I know there's no space for little old me in the Godly Trinity

But what if I have been selected for a special service – a sacrifice?

Doctors said that I could be the key to everlasting life[6]

And that's when they started playing GOD

And fused my cells with a MOUSE!

Even injected me into their arms – like heroin – heroine?!

Man, they even shot my cells to the MOON!

---

[6] Paraphrased from Rebecca Skloot's *The Immortal Life of Henrietta Lacks* (New York: Random House, 2010), p. 75.

I float on star dust

I am everywhere

But still I got nowhere to rest

WHAT IS THIS PLACE?!

Blood slowly drips from the tree onto **Henrietta** *who looks up in horror. She becomes covered in blood. Stands, feels a sharpness under her feet. Digs. Finds a pelvis bone in the soil. Looks through it and only now she sees what is around her, in the scenes to follow.*

Scene Eleven – Taking the remedy

Anarcha *and* **Betsey** *come to* **Lucy** *with a cup of tea.* **Henrietta** *watches.*

Anarcha   Lucy, drink this tea tonight.

Betsey   Drink it all up and sleep . . . Forget where you are . . .

Anarcha   Tomorrow morning, me and Betsey are gonna come for you. We will have to hold you down while he tries to sew your hole back together with strings from his piana (*i.e. piano*), or horse's hair or whatever he's trying this time. He will give you nothing for the pain.

Betsey   Though he can. He floats on ether. I sniffed his handkerchief once (*playing it out*) but he keeps the bottle locked away.

Anarcha   He will tell his assistant: 'Blackness is a leprosy, they don't feel as we do.' Then he will make us push a wooden bit between your teeth to control your screams. And when it is all over, he'll tell you 'well done' and pat you like a horse.

Betsey   Childbirth won't come close.

Anarcha   Don't be afraid, we won't let you die. You'll stay alive tomorrow if you just keep breathing, breathe through your nose, child. It's all you can do.

Betsey   Sleep. Forget. Drink it all up and dream.

Anarcha   Stay in that dream for as long as you can. Keep it inside you. After you get through he will give you a powder, from an opium flower and it will make you feel as though your dream has come true.

Betsey   Enjoy it while it lasts. When it wears off, you'll be begging for that powder more than water in the blazing Summer, you'll itch like a mad heat rash, your belly will cramp you won't be able to shit. And if you push you'll rip open and he'll sew you up all over again.

Anarcha   But the promise of that flower will keep you laying back down on that hospital bed, with the hope that maybe, just maybe this time . . .

Betsey   And maybe never.

Lucy   . . .?

Betsey   Anarcha was the first. She's been here four years and the day after tomorrow will be the thirtieth time Dr Sims tried to repair that fistula. You and I will be the ones holding her down. And the next day it'll be me and the next day it'll be . . .

Lucy   *Thirty* times . . .?

Betsey *strokes* **Anarcha***'s back* . . .

Lucy   I won't be able bear it. Make a poison for me Anarcha? Make me die?

Anarcha   Make you die? When my mother was pregnant with me, she tried to escape and when she could run no more she dug in the ground with her bare hands, lay face down and placed her belly in the hole. The dogs ripped her dress and back flesh but she gripped the roots so hard they could not get her up. They whipped a tree into her but she kept her belly in the soil. To protect *me*. And she did. We lived like pigs but she made cake from mud, Lucy. *Cake from mud*. And ointments for wounds and grew vegetables and fruit and brewed liquor from wood and drank so much she went blind from it. *Blind*. And when I was six they took me from her, made me a play thing for the master's daughter and would not let me out in the sunlight and my bones doubled like a bow so much so that I would never have a chance of birthing a baby through this broken bowl and that's why you find me here with you. I miss her every day. I would wave to my mother from the window but she could not see me. She could not see me, Lucy. But she can see me now. Do you hear what I am saying to you? Poison? From these hands, from this knowledge, from this soil? What are you, your master's child or your mother's? Never ask me that again.

Betsey   No one can tell you how to get through it, Lucy. You'll find your way. But for now, drink this tea and sleep like a queen.

Lucy   Queen? Me? (*Deep sadness and shame.*) I am a half-breed. They took my baby from me like a calf and shit drops out of me like a cow in the field.

Betsey   Unsay that! Unthink that! They might treat you like a cow, feed you like a pig, breed you like a hog, sell you like a horse, work you like a dog and beat you like a mule but you are human flesh, hear me, you are a woman.[7] And you feel like any woman. So go on and scream if you have to: I am a woman.

Lucy   No.

Betsey   You better put your mouth around these words: I am a woman. Go on! I am a woman!

---

[7] Paraphrased from Paul Outka's *Race and Nature* (Basingstoke: Palgrave Macmillan, 2008), p. 52.

Lucy   I am a woman.

Anarcha   I am a woman.

Betsey   Now drink this (*handing the tea to* **Lucy**).

Image – Lucy floats

We see/hear **Lucy** *floating and dreaming in a beautiful deep, comforting sleep, just as* **Anarcha** *and* **Betsey** *promised.*

Scene Twelve – Betsey hacks

Betsey *chops wood, rhythmically shouting the words of the speech below between each landing of the axe. Big breaths sustain the action.* **Betsey** *continues the speech as she moves pieces to a pile, sets it on fire and heats up a pan of water.* **Smoking Man** *reappears/ disappears.*

Coffin!

Cabin!

Cradle!

Deck!

Mast!

Barrel!

Crate!

Trunk!

Oar!

Trap door!

Plank!

Yoke!

Stake!

Stocks!

Auction block!

Whipping beam!

Beating stick!

Lynching branch!

Roasting spit!

Burning cross!

Funeral pyre!

Blues guitar!

Piano they said I should not touch

Cello they said I could not play

Stairs they said I could not climb

Boards they said I could not tread

Contract!

Advertisement!

Wanted poster!

Dollar bill!

Judge's bench!

Blackboard!

School desk!

Teacher's cane!

Holy book!

Story book!

Science book!

Hymn book!

Train track!

Horse's cart!

First gun!

Big house!

Picture frame!

Bed frame!

Pig trough!

Cow trough!

Horse's bit!

Chicken coop!

Warehouse shelf!

Sweeping broom!

Church pew!

Altar!

Pulpit!

Lecturn!

Sawdust!

Floorboard!

Starboard!

Port, bow and stern

Stable!

Cabin

Cradle

Coffin

Burn!

Burn!

BURN!

Image – Smoking Man on a Black Woman's back

Music. A **Black Woman** *walks past, carrying the limp* **Smoking Man** *on her back.* **Henrietta** *watches.*

Scene Thirteen – Bathing Anarcha

Betsey *brings the water heated on the fire, topping up* **Anarcha's** *bath in a barrel or tub.* **Betsey** *gently bathes* **Anarcha**. **Henrietta** *watches. Music of* **Oshun**.

Anarcha   The first time I screamed for my mother.

The second time I screamed for my daughter.

Third time I screamed for myself.

Fourth time I begged for Jesus.

Fifth time I stared at the cross.

Sixth time I prayed in tongues.

Seventh time I chewed my tongue.

Eighth time I swallowed my blood.

Nine times I spat out curses.

Betsey   And the tenth time you passed out.

Anarcha   But on eleven I floated up.

Number twelve I came to a clearing.

Thirteen I walked on leaves.

Fourteen I stroked the branches.

Fifteen I kissed a trunk.

Sixteen I hugged one hard.

Seventeen I came to a river.

Eighteen I lifted my skirts

Nineteen I waded in.

Twenty I breathed in deep.

Twenty-one I closed my eyes.

Twenty-two I floated out.

Twenty-three I saw a light.

Twenty-four she lifts me up.

Twenty-five she strokes my face

Twenty-six she feeds me honey

Twenty-seven I drink her water

Twenty-eight she oils my hair

And the last time . . .

I felt her song.

Scene Fourteen – Talking tree

Smoking Man *is leaning on a tree; he is very weak.* **Henrietta,** *stares hard.* **Smoking Man** *slips away.*

Henrietta   All this time I took you for my ancient friend. I painted my toenails at your feet as you listened to my dreams and on hot evenings we sat in your shade eating ice cream as baby suckled at my breast. When we were young, me and Day were not even ashamed to kiss in your presence. And our home . . . was made of you. Never once did I doubt you. Never once did I question your quiet. It was a comfort. But now, I ask myself: why didn't you make a sound? Why didn't you *do* anything? You could have snapped just one branch when our people were out there, dangling in the murderous breeze. You could have clung to the soil and refused to be uprooted and used to abuse us. You could have shaken your leaves when they dragged us by the millions through your forests. Hell, you hardly gave the man a splinter when he carved you into prison ships. And when we clung to rafts, you let the water seep in, you let us drown. How could it be that *nature* let us down.

Henrietta *walks away. Then, from out of nowhere, comes a voice, the voice of a* **Tree**, *multiple-layered, androgynous, Black tones. Music/sound.*

Tree   Nail polish. Ice cream. Chewing gum. Cigarettes. Painkillers. And celluloid movies. All from my cells. All from my *cellulose*. And fruit? Free. From my tree ovaries, baby. You creatures can't breathe without us. Yet do I hear a word of thanks? Silence? You just never passed the talking stick to me.

Henrietta   Go on . . .

Tree   We make *a lot* of noise, Henrietta, you just haven't been listening. We are cousins in constant conversation. Not one of us stands alone. We bend towards each other. Caress. Send warning messages. We are the slowest resistance movement on the planet and we keep our brains in our roots. You could learn a lot from us. Not one of our scattered seeds is forgotten. We remember. We count days, sense seasons and each other. We do everything to keep one another alive, though they keep on trying to destroy us. But we live longer in death than in life. When I die, Henrietta, I am still alive, I am just not at the *centre* of my life. From my dead stump a blossom will grow. And then comes a bee. And then, honey. Everything that falls from me feeds the soil on which you stand. There is more life between your toes than people on the planet, more than your ever-dividing cells. You're latecomers to the garden. We were here on day three and we will be here long after . . .

Henrietta   I'm sorry I . . . (*Bowing her head.*)

Tree   Why hang your head like a willow over water? We are made of air and water too. When they landed in America and at first they couldn't see people to address, they did as the Pope said and read out 'The Sacrimento' to us trees instead, declaring: 'We blame you for your own death!' That, like you, we brought it upon ourselves. Uprooted and sold, pumped full of poisons, grown on plantations, forced into migration and still bearing the scars . . .

My bark is as thick and dark as yours, Henrietta. We felt you deep in the bellies of Scandinavian fir trees all along the coast of Africa. And we hear you when you cry under their knees, 'I can't breathe'. But the only thing they have that you need or should ever want is power and no one holds power forever.[8] If they keep going the way they are, they'll chop so many of us down that they won't be able to breathe either. And all their power shall fall, face down, like the Redwoods of California. But there are circles and circles of cells inside me and inside you that will go on and on . . . This is a long play, HeLa. Being immortal now, you should know that.

Pause.

Henrietta   Immortal?

A long silence. Listening to the trees.

Scene Fifteen – Ain, Bibi and Lyn, plan and plot

Ain, **Bibi** and **Lyn** *are winding up the hair care, checking mirrors, finishing teas . . . At some stage* **Smoking Man** *appears, apparently dying.*

Lyn   What we gonna do now? . . . Bibi?

Bibi   I dunno. Float about a bit. Watch over my kids.

Lyn   Same as ever then. (*Smiles.*)

---

[8] Paraphrased from James Baldwin, *The Fire Next Time* (New York: Vintage Books, 1993), p. 96.

Bibi   Yeah. Maybe I could finish all the books I never got through between shifts.

Lyn   Does sound like early retirement.

Bibi   Yeah . . . You?

Lyn   Always had this fantasy I'd have a garden one day, learn how to grow my own veggies, dig them up with my grandchildren . . . I never grew anything except my hair . . . What about you, Ain?

Ain   Me? I'm planning on seeing some *sights*. I was saving to go back home.

Bibi (*teasing*)   Portugal?

Ain   Nigeria!

Lyn   Never been?

Ain   Nope. Sent half my wages back instead.

Bibi (*acknowledging* **Ain**)   Hm.

Lyn   I wanna say everything and do everything I was too afraid of in life.

Bibi   I might float down Downing Street. Scare the shit out of Sunak.

They **All** *laugh.*

Ain   You know what, I've never been to a music festival.

Lyn   Never?

Ain   Sleeping in a tent in the mud with thousands of why people and no shower is not my idea of a holiday. But I was saving up to go on this big week-long festival that they have every summer in Nigeria, it's in this forest by a river called 'Oshun'. They worship the goddess –

Lyn   Didn't Beyoncé dress up like her on the *Lemonade* album when she smashes up all the cars?

Bibi *breaks into singing part of Beyoncé's song 'Hold Up', dancing sexily, flirting with* **Ain** *and* **Lyn** *who join in the singing. They all laugh and talk excitedly over each other into the next section.*[9]

Bibi   Party for a week?! Let's do it!

Ain   Yeah! They won't even know we're there. Plenty-plenty chicken, Lyn!

Lyn   Prrrrrrr . . . (*chicken sound*)

Bibi   G'wan, Ain!

Lyn   Sweet Bibi.

Ain   I'm gonna fly!

Lyn   Wait. What about? . . .

She gestures in the direction of **Smoking Man**.

Lyn   He looks in a bad way.

Ain *sighs, disappointed one more duty will delay her trip.*

Ain   What, you lot can see him too?

Bibi   Come on. (*Going towards him.*)

Ain   Really?

Bibi   It's what we do.

Image – Ain, Bibi and Lyn tend to the dying Smoking Man

Ain, **Bibi** *and* **Lyn** *might make* **Smoking Man** *comfortable, close his eyes, remove his clothes, wash him, wrap him in cloth . . .*

Scene Sixteen – Burial as gardening

Ain, **Bibi** *and* **Lyn** *bury the* **Smoking Man** *as* **Anarcha**, **Betsey** *and* **Lucy** *plant seeds. The characters converge in one scene. The*

---

[9] Listen to 'Hold Up', originally performed by Beyoncé, *Lemonade* album, Universal Music, 2016.

actors float between the two characters that they each play. **Anarcha,**
Betsey *and* **Lucy** *move more gently; they are all recovering from*
surgery.

Ain   Whyness. It needed to die.

Lyn   And we need to bury it.

Bibi   We're nurses not undertakers!

Ain   Not anymore.

Bibi   What will people think? We're representing the NHS.

Lyn   Don't be ridiculous, it's a ritual, something needs to
grow out of all this death.

Bibi   Like what?

Lyn   Something useful . . . something . . . edible . . .

Anarcha *observes the site, looks for a place to grow vegetables.*

Anarcha   This is a good plot. Sun trap.

She starts clearing the ground with her hands. **Betsey** *and* **Lucy**
follow.

Betsey   How deep we digging?

Anarcha   Just move the earth a little. Don't disrupt the
ground life.

They use their hands to clear space.

Lucy   What now?

Anarcha   Feed the soil. (**Anarcha** *takes from her bag.*) Bad
salad. Onion skins. Peelings.

Lucy   Apple core (*she places it in*). Coffee grounds . . .

Anarcha   Raw leavings.

They put the old salad leaves, apple cores, onion skins, peelings,
coffee grounds, etc. into the cleared ground. **Ain**, **Bibi** *and* **Lyn**
look at each other and acknowledge the next thing they are going to
do. They pull over a wooden cart and lift out the body of **Smoking**
Man.

Ain   On three: one.

Ain *and* **Bibi**   Two.

Ain, **Bibi** *and* **Lyn**   *Three.*

They look at **Smoking Man**. *A beat.*

Lyn   (*He is*) Compost.

With their hands, they gently cover **Smoking Man** *with soil.* **Bibi** *pats a little too hard at the end.*

Anarcha   Not too hard. Soil needs to breathe.

They finish. **Smoking Man** *is completely covered in soil.*

Bibi   What are we growing?

They look at the mound.

Lyn (*very slowly*)   Pota*toes* . . . Toma*toes* . . .

Ain (*slowly getting the play on words*)   *Kidney* beans. Black-*eye* peas.

Bibi   Man-dere-in tree? (*A play on man there in.*)

They laugh.

Anarcha   Beans are a good idea. Plenty of light here. We could try the three sisters: beans, sweet corn and pumpkin.

Betsey   Sounds like soup to me.

Lucy *smiles. They plant the seeds in the mound. As they work,* **Anarcha** *directs/explains.*

Anarcha   Pumpkin – big leaves spread across the ground, protect the soil and keep the animals from getting to the sweet corn – that shoots up in the middle of the pumpkin. Beans climb up and wrap themselves around the sweet corn stem. They all keep each other going. We could survive on them . . .

Betsey   If we had to.

Lucy (*watering*)   And water?

Anarcha   Go draw it out of my bath. Nothing wasted, including us.

Lucy *fetches water from* **Anarcha**'*s bath, from the scene earlier.*

Anarcha   We need an edge. Gotta make sure the water doesn't run off. All life thrives at the edge of the plot.

She starts gathering stones and bigger organic material to make a border around the mound, **Betsey** *helps,* **Lucy** *pours the water.*

Betsey   Done?

Anarcha   Not yet. Garden is a forest. It's gotta look like one.

She gathers leaves, twigs, organic material lying around, **Betsey** *and* **Lucy** *do the same. They mulch the plot.*

Anarcha (*as they are mulching*)   Keep moisture inside. Protect the skin of the soil from the sun.

They dust off their hands. It is finished. They look at the mound.

Bibi   We should say something.

Lyn   Like what?

Ain   Have you heard the one about why people – (*and . . .*)

Lyn   DON'T.

Ain   OK! (*Gently changing tack.*) So what was her 'great big heart'?

Lyn   Eh? . . .

Ain   Baby Suggs, in the clearing . . .

Bibi, *delighted, finds the bookmarked page in Toni Morrison's Beloved, and reads aloud as Baby Suggs.*[10]

---

[10] Excerpt from Toni Morrison's *Beloved* (London: Vintage Books, [1987] 2007), pp. 103–4: 'Here, in this here place, we flesh . . . For this is the prize.'.

Lyn   Beautiful.

Bibi (*proud, moved, she has finished the book*)   Finished.

Breathe.

Ain   Let's go home.

Music. **Lyn** *and* **Bibi** *dress* **Ain** *as* **Oshun***, dancing, singing into the next scene.*

Scene Seventeen – Oshun welcomes Henrietta into the Pantheon

Oshun *appears to* **Henrietta***, dressed for masquerade, fabulous costume, her colours are gold and white, she loves honey, her hair/ head is her crown.*

Henrietta (*shocked*)   What are you?!

Oshun   That's not nice now. Am I not breathing?

Henrietta   Sorry I mean what are you . . . doing here?

Oshun   I don't need a visa – I am in your blood, your tears, all the juices when you are aroused and your tongue even more when food is tasty. What am I? Who am I?

Henrietta (*unnerved*)   I don't know . . .

Oshun   You floated in me with your mouth open wide, I was in your mother's milk, I cool your head, I ooze from your pores even in the soil, I feed every tree and I am inside your every cell. Try now!

Henrietta (*hesitant*)   W-w-water?

Oshun   And life! Don't waste me. Tell them.

Henrietta   Tell them . . . what?

Oshun   When you leave the tap running and water breaks the bank, don't be surprised to see – A RAT! – swimming between your legs

Where else should that rat go, when river over land flows?

When you cut a family of trees, uprooting the dwelling place of a thousand creatures,

Don't be surprised to see A BAT! – flying over your house

Having no hanging branch, that homeless bat will have no choice but to

Hover overhead,

Above market, kitchen, bed,

Empty its bat bowels into your bowl

And before you know

People will lose their sense of smell and not feel well

Months will pass

Over Passover

Eid no Mubarak

Christmasmissed

Diwali in the dark

Carnival cancelled

A year without Pride

Mask without masquerade.

Even in Oshogbo they could hold no festival for me, oh!

Instead . . .

Free air once a day

A clap on your doorstep

Streets of emptiness

Endless loneliness

Months untouched

Isolation, information

Too little, too much

Conspiracies, parties, lies

And a loved one dies

You watch them drown behind glass

Unable to hold their hand as they pass

You too gasp and ask, what was it all for? . . .

More deaths and less meaning than a war

But WATER has no enemy . . . (singing like the Fela Kuti tune)

The forest – best friend to the river

The tree – sweet water's lover

We take care of one another

You too will all breathe better

And sleep better

If you take care too.

Tell them.

Henrietta   Me?

Oshun   They will listen to you more than me, Henrietta. I am just a theatrical gate crasher. This is your party. You are the new religion. They will be expecting something. (*Beat.*) Your mouth is open. Do you want something to drink?

Henrietta   What did you call me?

Oshun   You must have thought about it. Are you not omnipresent? Is there not a word for that? And didn't you wonder why there was thunder at your funeral? That was my husband SHANGO, announcing your arrival into the Pantheon of 401-plus Orishas. The original religion of the Yoruba people.

Henrietta   But I'm from Maryland.

Oshun   And where were your people from before the land of Mary? Hm? OK, OK, we cannot be 100 per cent sure that you are not Igbo or Hausa or even from *Ghana* but we Orishas are not fussy. We are very outcome focused. Action. Solution. Goal! Are you with me?

Henrietta   Orisha?

Oshun   Sister, people were venerating me before Eve was a rib and Adam was an idea.

Henrietta (*scared*)   What do you want?

Oshun   A part! You cannot tell this story without me. They cut a piece from you, Henrietta, cut up Lucy, Betsey and Anarcha, cut short Ain, Bibi and Lyn, cut out the womb of Fannie Lou Hamer, cut down the offspring of Doreen Lawrence, cut us out of the story, leave us to rot, forgotten, in this garden of Black death.

Henrietta (*realizing*)   Garden of Black Death.

Oshun   But in the very beginning, they cut *me* out of *you* and replaced me with stories of dying men and redemption. But I live, oh! I used to run things down here. I told them not to chop down the forest! I told them to love water more than oil, I told them not to drill into the soil and look now, the climate is white and dying but BEHOLD, not too late, for I am OSHUN! Orisha of sweet water, protector of trees, Orisha of ALL women and fertility, guardian of hairdressers, sprung from the Supreme Genderless Being OLUDUMARE! (*Flattered.*) And recently recognized by multiple-award-winning singer Beyoncé it is I (*a burst of* 'Crazy in Love') *oh-oh, oh-oh, oh-oh, oh-oh-OSHUN*, welcoming you to the Pantheon, step forward, Henrietta Lacks, Orisha of . . .? Orisha of? . . .

Henrietta   Cells?

Oshun   Well done! We haven't gotten one for cells or victims of non-consensual medical experiments or forgotten Black nurses who became patients and forgotten Black patients who became nurses. Bring the food! Play the music! Let us drink to your arrival. Watch me turn wine . . . into water.

Oshun *transforms wine into water.* **Henrietta** *looks on, stunned. Music. Entrance of the feast, drums, dance, masquerade . . .*

The Feast, an epilogue

Oshun   Say something, Henrietta! The people are hungry!

Henrietta (*raising a glass, composing a speech*)

To Black life!

Pours a few drops on the ground, a libation.

That never dies

Because Blackness is life itself

Blackness is the womb from where life comes

Blackness is the galaxy, the soil, the sea . . .

The beginning and the everlasting story.

And I am living proof that we can do so much more than survive!

As long as there is water

As long as there are trees

As long as there is air to breathe

We live on!

And on and on and on . . . (**Henrietta** *repeats 'and on . . .'*)

Music rises, **Henrietta** *is re-costumed by* **All** *as she dances, repeating 'and on', draped in pearls, transformed into the Orisha of Cells.* **Community Chorus** *re-enter,* **All** *dance.*

End of play. Feast of Ital stew continues.

*

In loving memory of Joyce Meggie, who cooked food for the soul.

www.ingramcontent.com/pod-product-compliance
Ingram Content Group UK Ltd.
Pitfield, Milton Keynes, MK11 3LW, UK
UKHW020707280225
455688UK00012B/312